AF425236

The Letter A

Color in the object that start with the letter "a".

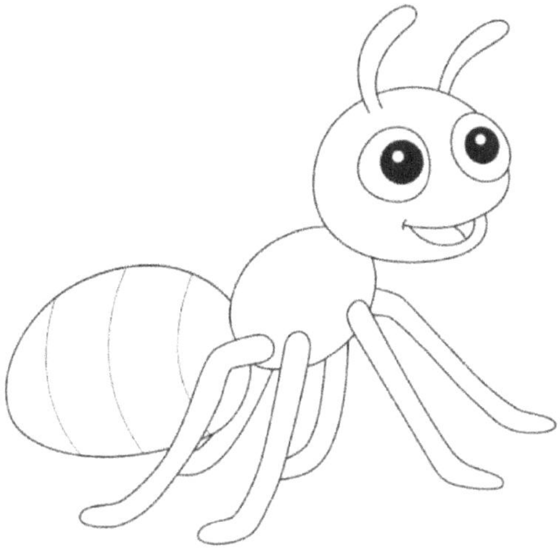

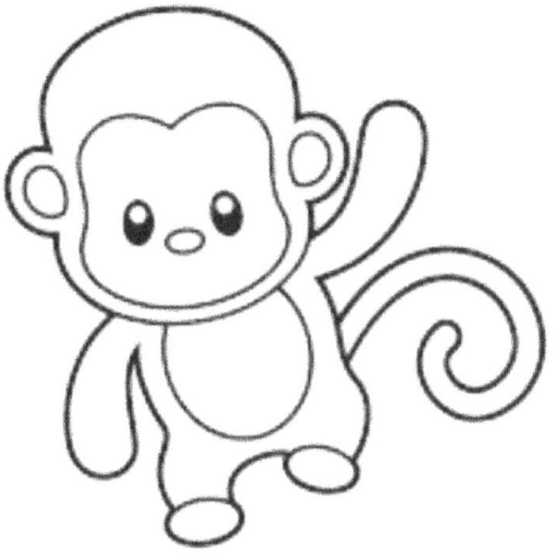

Aa

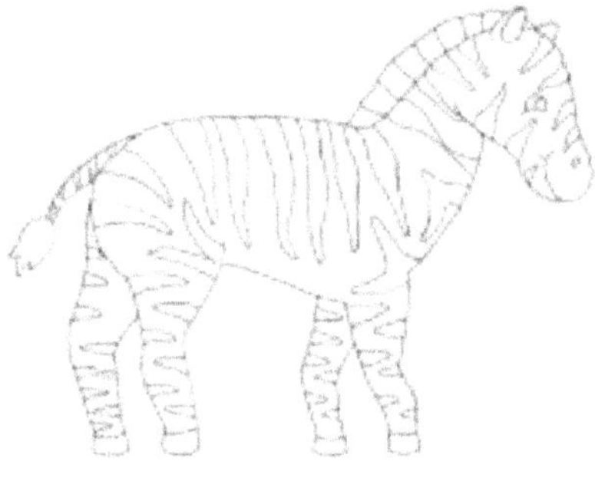

The Letter B

Color in the object that start with the letter "b".

The Letter C

Color in the object that start with the letter "c".

The Letter D

Color in the object that start with the letter "d".

The Letter E

Color in the object that start with the letter "e".

The Letter F

Color in the object that start with the letter "f".

The Letter G

Color in the object that start with the letter "g".

The Letter H

Color in the object that start with the letter "h".

The Letter I

Color in the object that start with the letter "i".

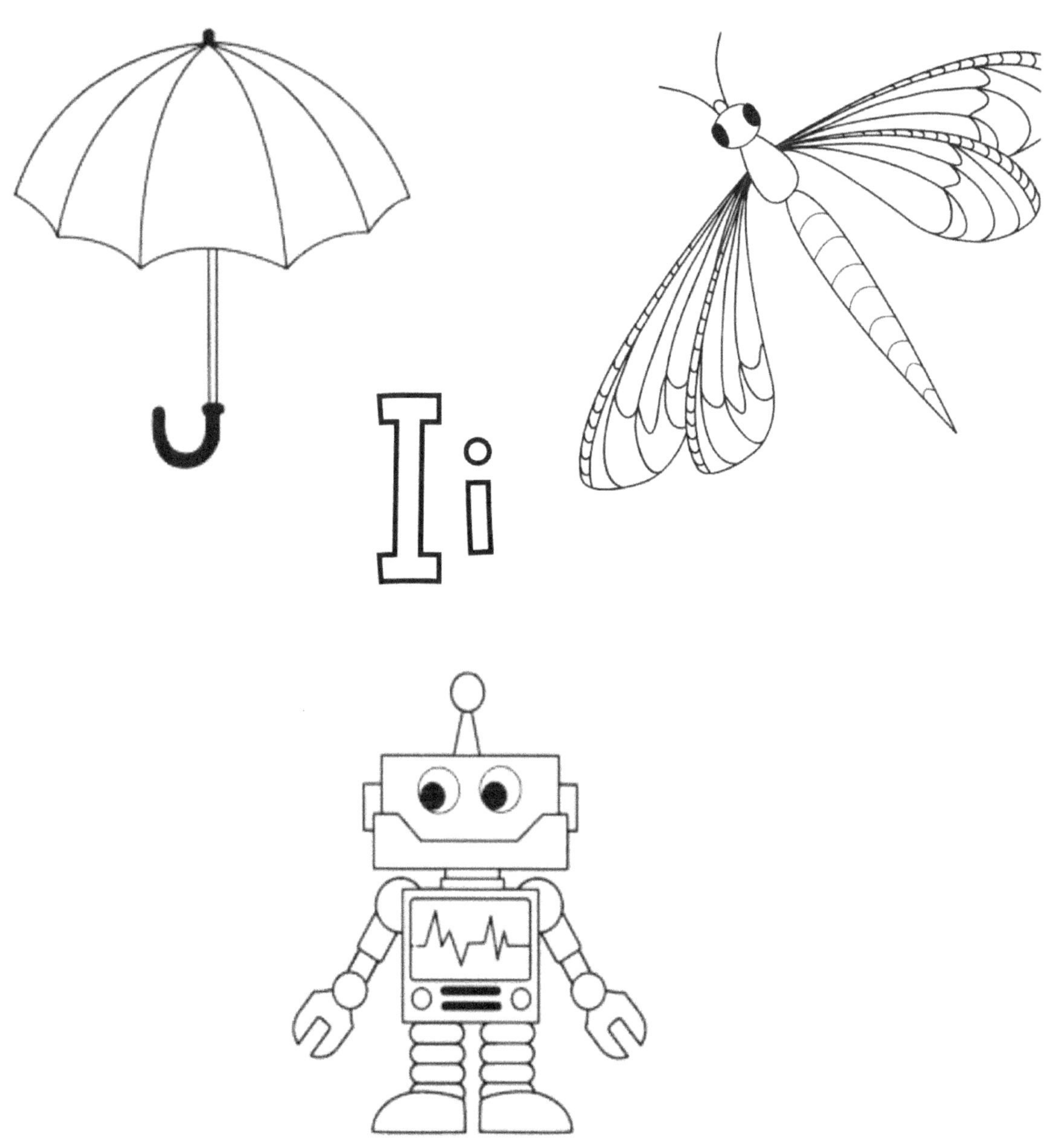

The Letter J

Color in the object that start with the letter "j".

The Letter K

Color in the object that start with the letter "k".

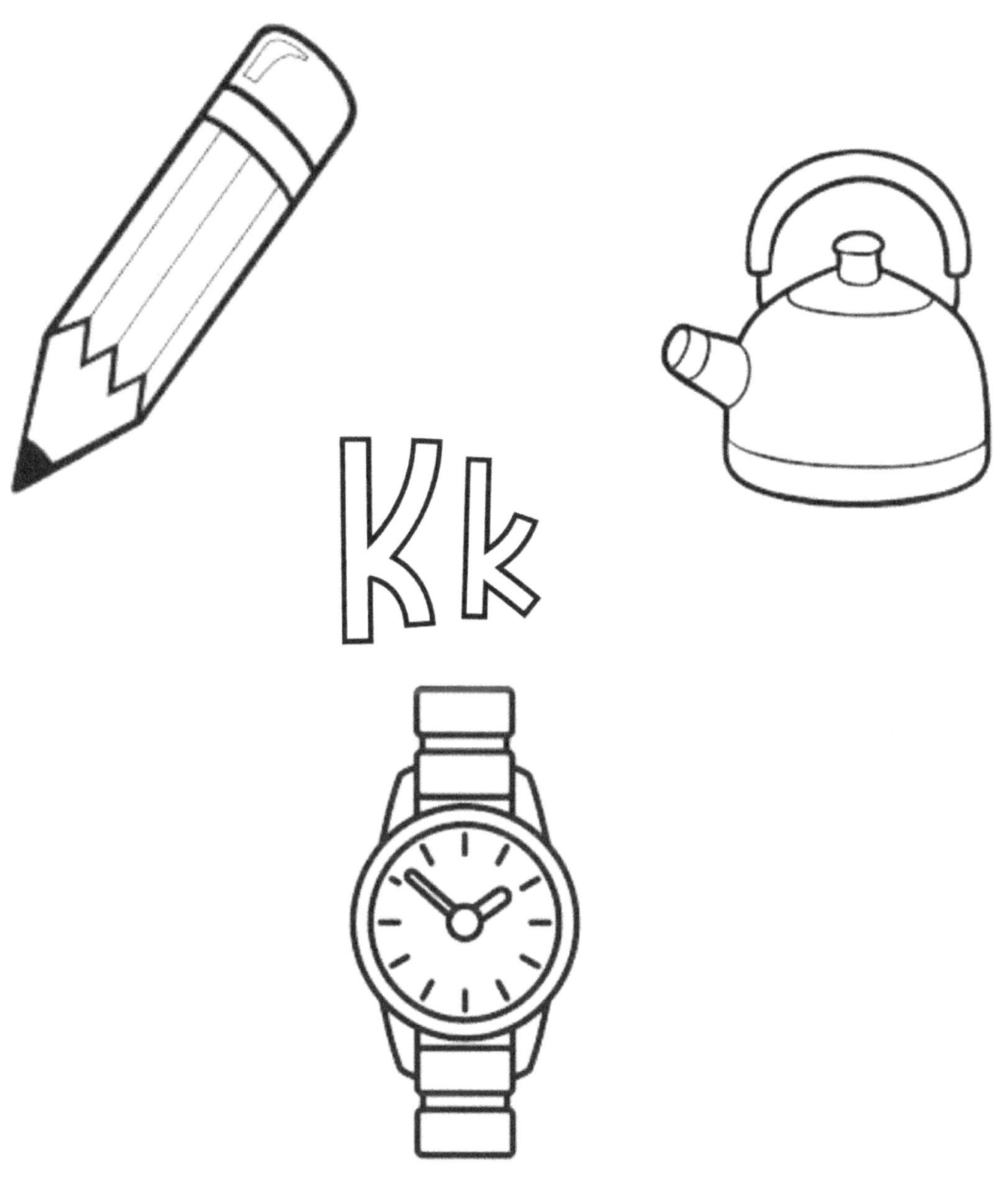

The Letter L

Color in the object that start with the letter "l".

The Letter M

Color in the object that start with the letter "m".

The Letter N

Color in the object that start with the letter "n".

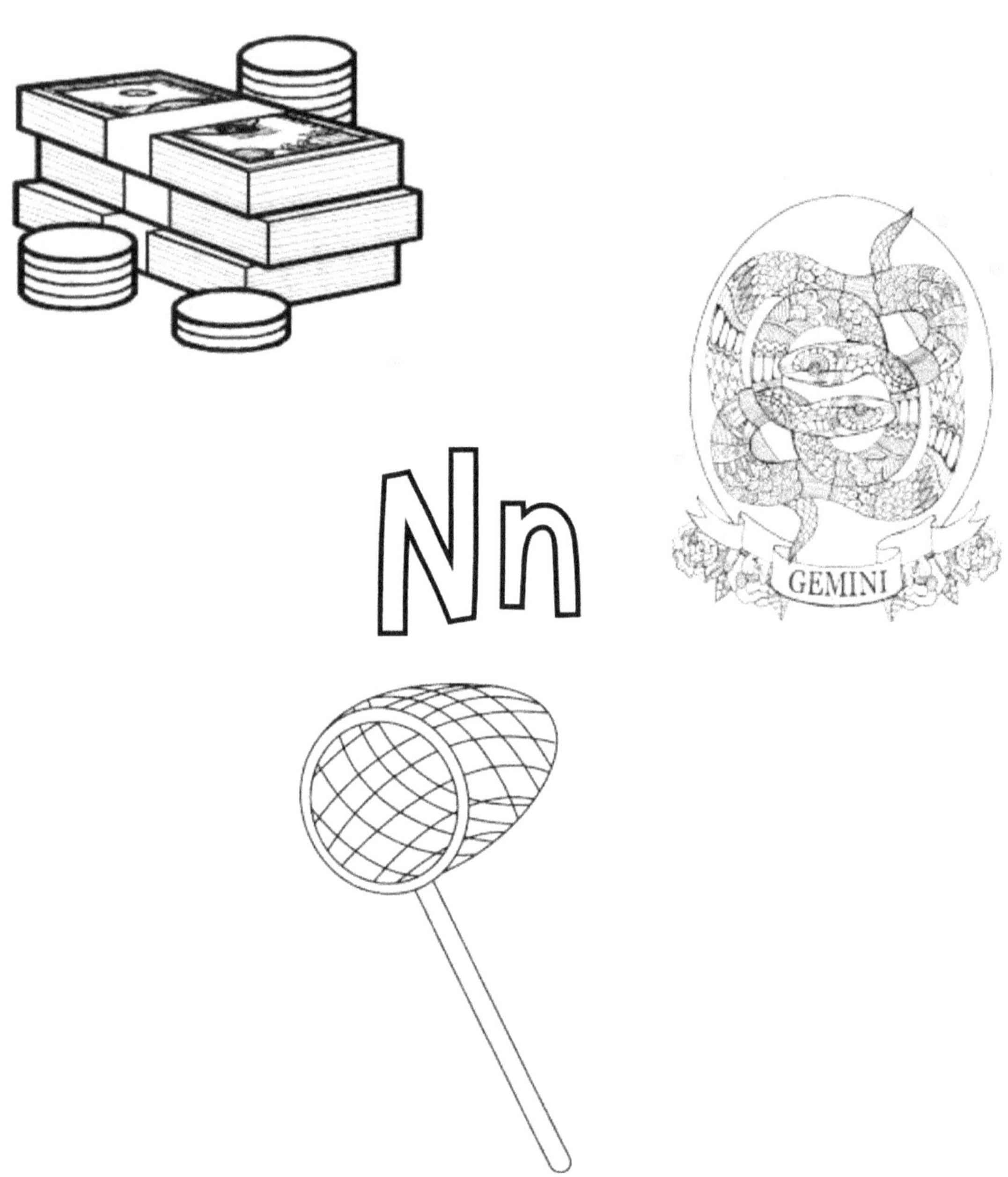

The Letter O

Color in the object that start with the letter "o".

The Letter P

Color in the object that start with the letter "P".

The Letter Q

Color in the object that start with the letter "q".

The Letter R

Color in the object that start with the letter "r".

The Letter S

Color in the object that start with the letter "s".

The Letter T

Color in the object that start with the letter "t".

The Letter U

Color in the object that start with the letter "u".

The Letter V

Color in the object that start with the letter "v".

The Letter W

Color in the object that start with the letter "w".

The Letter X

Color in the object that start with the letter "x".

The Letter Y

Color in the object that start with the letter "y".

The Letter Z

Color in the object that start with the letter "z".